I Am Here

THE HEALING JOURNEY

OF CAREGIVING

Kevin Sharpe

ISBN: 1-4700-7809-0
ISBN-13: 9781470078096

To my parents,
Joan and Joe,
who have always been here,
caring for me.

Contents

Introduction

The inner landscape

As I started thinking about writing this book, I kept feeling a tremendous tenderness welling up in my heart. It really gave me pause – not because tenderness is foreign to me, but because there was such a paradoxical quality to it. There was a particular strength within it. It felt full and whole. It was curious enough to give me pause.

Looking at this new expression of tenderness more closely, I found that it was not just on the surface, but grew deep and robustly. It had become the ground of my inner landscape, all those peaks and valleys of my emotions and feelings and non-physical aspects of myself. This was a strange and welcome awareness for me after the last 15 months of life as a full-time caregiver – a time when my inner landscape was often fractured, sharp, and jagged in the way fear and anxiety of the unknown can cause it to be.

Now I realize that this new tenderness forms the lens through which I view and live life. It's like new growth that reclaims the scorched earth after a wildfire: vibrant, pliable, and bursting with life. This tenderness bears witness to how my caregiving journey with my father and my mother has transformed me, healed me. Tenderness is my strength. Its quality infuses most every part of my life.

By extension, this is a book born out of that tenderness. It shines light on a tender, holistic way of providing care. This may sound redundant to some. I believe, however, that anyone who has had life turned upside down by the sudden shift into the role of being a caregiver, particularly a caregiver of someone who is critically ill, understands how the quality of tenderness can quickly become like an endangered species, always on the verge of extinction. There are so many things continually calling for attention that all can rapidly become overwhelming, often turning the caregiver into someone more akin to a task master or a drill sergeant. It can frequently leave us feeling numb, or angry, or rigid, or anything but tender.

Ultimately caregiving is a healing spirit. It can transform both the caregiver and the person receiving care.

We need only open to it, agree to let it move us into our inner landscape. This is where we connect with that healing spirit, where it helps us touch ground, where it helps us touch heart. This is the way that strengthens, and softens, and heals, allowing us to be okay with being vulnerable and unsure of the next step or of what tomorrow will bring.

And so in the following pages, we explore this way that takes us into our inner landscape, the realm of our own healing journey. It is here where we'll find five aspects of caregiving, each serving as a guide for this journey. These aspects have the potential to bring us consciously into the love that always surrounds us and holds us – particularly in the middle of something so profound, so big, and so intimate as is the act of giving care to the one we love.

There is a particular exterior reality for most who are active caregivers. This reality can seem always to be teetering on the edge of caving in or of taking on a crushing intensity, with no relief in sight. When will it stop? That question was often on my lips. When will it stop? When will it stop? When will it stop? When will it stop? When will it stop? During the first eight months of my caregiver's life, it became a mantra, repeated on some level almost constantly. I suppose it was my hope that by saying it over and over and over that I'd somehow get an answer. As we'll see, it was the wrong question to be asking.

In the exterior reality, friends do become silent, fading into their day-to-day lives. Community becomes a common casualty – one that, in turn, breeds isolation, which only adds to the intensity of life. When someone does remember to call or does stop us in the store and asks how we are or what we're doing now, what can we say?

I want to say: "I've been hurting so much and have been so exhausted. Life has been like a flood washing over me for the past many months of my father's illness, of his pain, of his delirium, of his sleepless nights, of his hospital stay after hospital stay, of his too many ambulance rides, of his too many doctors, of his pain, of his weight loss, of his losing the ability to walk, of his no appetite, of his pain, of his procedure after procedure, of his not being able to eat, of his dehydration, of his chemo, of his radiation, of his pain."

Of course, I don't say this. I can't. Part of the reason I want to answer this way is because I want someone to *understand* what my life is like now. I also know that words really can't express my experience nor make anyone actually understand when I can't even understand it all. This is *my* experience and part of that experience is not having the words to communicate fully how I feel, how life has been for me, and what I'm actually doing day in and day out.

And so, the isolation continues to expand, the intensity to build.

There is a wordless truth, though, under all of this intensity of life that a caregiver slowly begins to sense. It's wordless, I figure, because it's a truth that is simply too big for words. Initially, we most often become aware of it in the times in between all the activities, in the brief moments of pause that unfold when we're really present.

For me, this truth expresses itself as feelings surfacing from a deep knowing that all of my caregiving experiences are more profound and powerful and healing and bigger-than-me than I can ever fully comprehend from this side of reality. Knowing and feeling and living this, however, gives me strength – strength to continue showing up, strength to continue opening the door to my parents' house each morning, and strength to walk inside again and again and say: "I am here."

My brother and I split each 24-hour period.

He takes the night from about 8:30 p.m.
until 8:30 a.m.

I take the day shift from 8:30 a.m. until
about 8:30 p.m.

1

I am here
for you

As I get out of my car each morning at my parents' house, I try to notice the openness and freshness of the outside. All of the world is going about its living of life. On any given morning the birds are singing, the grass and trees are growing, the wind is gently blowing, the sun is rising, and my father is dying. I pause at the bottom of the few steps leading up to the front door. Here is where I take a deep breath, say a short prayer – for strength, for presence, for understanding, for a smile on my face.

Now I open the door and walk in.

My father is reclined in his chair, waiting for me. The pain keeps his sleep at bay most nights. If sleep does come, it's for short pieces of time. He tries to sleep in the bed next to my mother, his wife of 56 years. But for some reason, he usually can't make it through the night in their bed. The pain is too severe when he tries to lie on his back. No one understands why this is happening. No one, not even the doctors. But he tries. He likes to be next to her.

My mother, who has her own health problems brought on by breast cancer, lymphedema, and 45 or so years of rheumatoid arthritis, shares with me one morning what has become a ritual of sorts for my father. In the early morning around 5:00 a.m., if my father is in their bed, he asks my mother a simple question: Is Kevin here yet? "No, Joe, he's not here yet. He'll be here in a little while." So he says to her, "I'm going to get up and wait for him."

He then slowly gets up and navigates his walker into the living room to his chair by the front door. Of course, those nights when he can't even get into the bed because of the pain, he spends napping and waiting in the chair for morning and, I suppose, for me.

Perhaps the most easily recognizable role of any active caregiver is the role of I-am-here-for-you, the role of performing the day-to-day minutia of things. It's odd how these things become less distinct and almost invisible to those looking on from a distance – healthcare providers, friends, even family. Each of the activities, though, for the caregiver doing them tends to come together to form a sort of quick-tempoed litany for the day.

For me it was a litany of preparing and giving medications, cleaning and putting ointments on my father's bed sores, getting hot washcloths to wash his face, getting cold washcloths to help with nausea, dressing and undressing him, washing and brushing his hair, shaving him, trimming his nose hairs, clipping his finger and toe nails, preparing the line-up of drinks to try to hydrate him, preparing meals that he may not even eat, trying to get him to drink and eat (please), helping with going to the bathroom, wiping the drool from his chin again and again, arranging pillows, taking blood pressure readings, counting calories.

The litany goes on, of course, and also shifts more to the outside world as the day unfolds. There is the shopping, trying to find food that can be eaten without teeth, searching for food that has high calorie and protein counts, getting prescriptions filled, going to the bank, paying bills, making appointments with his long list of doctors, getting to the appointments, getting home and settled again, continually trying to find doctors who may be able to diagnose what is going on in my father's body (why is he so sick and getting sicker), describing an ever-growing list of symptoms to my father's doctors because of his increasing difficulty with talking. being my father's advocate with the doctors (please, doctor, please remember that my father is a person and really does have feelings, emotions, and is in incredible pain).

Regularly the litany changes to incorporate new things. Now there is the part that involves the walker. Later there is the part that involves the wheel chair and the bedside commode. Later still, there is the part that involves buying diapers, changing diapers, wiping my father, buying many more diapers. Eventually the litany grows to include the delivery of the hospital bed to the house, buying sheets for the hospital bed, buying blankets.

And then there is the odd, sublime aspect of the litany that involves the not-doing (anymore): the not helping my father sit up on the side of the hospital bed (anymore) because it hurts him too much, the not hearing my father form words (anymore) because his muscles are failing, the not seeing the hospital bed empty (anymore) because he's so weak he can't move from it (anymore).

Then that moment arrives ushering in the final strange not-doing of the litany: the not seeing my father in the bed anymore. Ever again. The not seeing my father anymore. Ever again.

And the litany comes to an end.

The Job Description

Being there for the person we're caring for is essentially the job description of the caregiver. The person who needs our care needs us to show up – needs us to be there *for* her or him. This person needs us to do or to assist in the activities that will get her or him through the physical part of living life.

This is the part of caregiving that most people easily understand, even if only intellectually. They get that medicine has to be administered, baths have to be given, food has to be prepared, pillows have to be adjusted, etc. It is the part of caregiving that is most often needed by the person being cared for. In short, this most physical aspect of caregiving is the primary external constant and the initial way caregiving unfolds.

The Caregiver's Healing Journey

The days and nights of caregiving can become filled to overflowing with the details of I-am-here-for-you. The caregiver somehow finds a way, though, to manage them – either by moxie, miracle, or magic. As care becomes more involved, as it becomes more hands-on, a near-constant flow of adrenaline seems to support the movements of hands and feet that are always doing, doing, doing, going, going, going. It can quickly become all-consuming.

Understandably enough, all of this I-am-here-for-you may begin to take a toll on the caregiver. This toll can show up in the caregiver's body as exhaustion, stress, mental as well as physical pain, often leading to the caregiver's own set of health concerns.

For as physically challenging as this aspect of caregiving can be, it is significant – and not just for the person receiving care. I-am-here-for-you is significant because all the *doing* and all the *going* get us out of our heads and into our bodies in a very real way. This being in our bodies has the potential to take us to a threshold of sort, a deeper aspect of the caregiver's journey where we are offered an opportunity to move into a liminal space of transformation and authentic healing. Of course, we're not obligated to take this deeper journey. If we do, however, we caregivers find that it's not a journey that uniquely takes place in our exterior world. It is a journey that moves us through our inner landscape – an intimate world that is usually quite foreign to most.

The Inner Landscape

The inner landscape is a vibrant, fully alive, continuous environment that we can enter into any time we choose to. For some, however, hearing the phrase *inner landscape* can create some confusion. In part, it's because the phrase is not all that common in most circles of conversations. The fact that we can't touch or see or hear the inner landscape with our physical senses doesn't help matters much. But it's worth remembering that this non-physical landscape has a direct and tangible impact on our physical, day-to-day lives. That alone is reason enough to become more familiar with our inner landscapes: all those peaks and valleys of our emotions and feelings and non-physical aspects of ourselves.

Pause

To gain entry to the inner landscape in a supportive way, we only need to pause. It's a simple thing – taking a pause. It is also an important step that can seem to be insurmountable because of all the doing and going of providing care. I know this. I lived this. But it isn't insurmountable. Taking a pause only has to take a few minutes. Even a few moments can provide enough time to have a supportive experience of our inner landscape. A deep breath or two in through the nose and exhaled through the mouth is all it takes to create the pause that starts to open the space of our inner landscape.

Taking an intentional pause also invokes our awareness. And it's with our awareness that we move through our inner landscape. Awareness is that quality which allows us to be present to what's happening. With awareness in hand, we're ready to shift more fully into our own inner landscape.

The Shift

It is an interesting paradox that is worth remembering now and throughout the healing journey of caregiving: Our inner landscape which exists in that non-physical realm of our emotions and feelings and mind directly impacts our physical body and our physical experience. This paradox points towards the connection that exists between our physical body and our non-physical mind. Because each influences the other, it stands to reason that we can access our mind – our inner landscape – through our physical body. This is why the I-am-here-for-you aspect of caregiving is often the gateway into our inner landscape: It gets us to that entry point in a supportive, focused way. It gets us out of our intellect and into our body.

Once we're in our physical body in a very real way and have made a conscious pause, we can make the shift from external experience to the experience of our inner landscape. We make this shift quite naturally and quite frequently throughout our day. Yet we often aren't aware that we're shifting into our inner landscape. The difference between all those shift experiences and what we're working with now all comes down to awareness, which we've empowered through our conscious pause. This is the element that allows us to shift and also remain present to whatever we discover in our inner landscape. It becomes a powerful tool for our journey. It actually allows us to dive below the surface of our caregiving experiences in order to be with them and learn as well as heal from them.

Once we have made the shift into our inner landscape, what is it that we are actually looking for? What do we do? The first step is to maintain our awareness of what is actually happening from moment to moment. The second step is to become aware of any and all sensations. Sensation is the equivalent of the language or voice of our inner landscape.

When we hear the word *sensation*, most of us will immediately think of physical sensation. However, we need to expand our definition of this idea. While it's true that a sensation can be physical – like an itch or a pain – a sensation can also be an emotion or a feeling. It can be a memory or a story or an image in our mind's eye. It might be a voice or a sound we hear in our mind. In short, a sensation can be anything we experience in our body or our mind, either physical or non-physical. It is through sensation, in whichever form it takes, that we see and hear and explore our inner landscape.

My brother and I split each 24-hour period.

He takes the night from about 8:30 p.m. until 8:30 a.m.

I take the day shift from 8:30 a.m. until about 8:30 p.m.

2

I am here
for me

The day is over. My shift is over. I'm beat.

I have a few crackers with some cheese. A late night snack really. It's what my supper on any given night has transformed into. It seems to do. Anymore I'm always too tired to cook let alone eat a real dinner.

As I get into bed, I put the handsets to my landline phone and my cell phone on the nightstand next to my bed. I make sure they're lined up, well charged, and in easy reach. They're my constant companions while I'm in my house, always ready for a call to move into action. On average I seem to be getting about one of this kind of call per month. It's enough to keep me on edge.

Planning - always be
for how to be there
"in case"

I turn on the small lamp next to my bed. Then I check to make sure its bulb is secure. The lamp stays on all night. Total darkness seems too much anymore – too suffocating, too scary.

It's crazy – this phone-and-lamp ritual before bed. But it brings some order into my life. It gives me something to hold onto, something I can actually control.

At this point (it's been about four months now), I'd really like to be able to just fall asleep and then sleep soundly through the night. Instead of good sleep, though, I get thoughts. They sound like this tonight:

> Day after day after day after day after day
> after day after day after day after day after
> day after day after day after day after day ...

These kinds of thoughts swirl around my mind. Sometimes they're loud and rowdy. Sometimes they're low and murmuring. They are, however, most always there.

Even the brief periods of time that have become my only me-time – those few moments between my lying down in bed at night and my drifting off to sleep or between my sleep and my sitting up in bed to start the day – even these brief periods of time aren't completely mine. Often they get invaded, like right now when I'm aware of the endless stretch of no-more's: no more sleeping late in the morning, no more days off, no more days just for me to do whatever I want, no more vacations, no more day trips, no more evenings out, no more life for me, no more of *my* life.

In the space of a few seconds, these thoughts have me on a slippery slope. They crowd my mind. I get caught up in the story line. All of a sudden, my me-time quickly collapses in on itself.

It's not a good way to end an exhausting day. It's not a good way to start an already too full day. It's just not good at all, but it is thoroughly real. It is thoroughly human. And it's okay.

Landing in Ourselves

Whenever life isn't lining up with our idea of how it should be, we experience stress. Let's face it. As an active caregiver, rarely is there a day that goes by during which this scenario doesn't unfold, during which we don't find ourselves face-to-face with stress. It was one of my most intimate companions when I was caring for my father.

The more wrapped up in the I-am-here-for-you aspect of caregiving we become, the more we usually neglect the I-am-here-for-me of caregiving. The result often ends up being a decrease in our ability to be with the stress of caregiving in a way that doesn't harm us. Turning towards

I-am-here-for-me instead of avoiding it is vital to managing the stress.

It is through this aspect of I-am-here-for-me that we're brought face-to-face with a fact we often ignore: We are only human. Becoming a caregiver has not transformed us into an omnipotent god. That may sound farfetched. "Of course," the intellect may say, "I know that I'm not an all-powerful god."

However, an exploration of the inner landscape of I-am-here-for-me can reveal truths about ourselves that our intellects often go to extreme lengths to deny or to distort.

Within the I-am-here-for-me inner landscape, we can discover the truths of the enormously important all-too-human side of ourselves: our bodies, our emotions, our reactions, our projections, our motivations. It's within the inner landscape of this aspect where we also have the opportunity to finally get real with ourselves about ourselves, about the situation, and about our relationship to the situation.

On the Surface With I-Am-Here-For-Me

As caregivers, we may hear one single line of well intentioned advice more often than others: You have to take care of yourself. This is a truth that most caregivers do understand. How we, as caregivers, actually work with this truth of needing to take care of ourselves is often the conundrum and the start of the pattern of turning away from the fact that we are only human.

This situation is one of the dynamics that may live on the surface of I-am-here-for-me. Dynamics like these can be daunting. They can be overwhelming. They can seem impossible to navigate, regardless of how much we'd like to jump into taking care of ourselves or remembering that we are only human. Unfortunately they become all-too-familiar, always shutting us down to I-am-here-for-me, always bringing us to a standstill in front of the same two roadblocks: either not having enough time or not having enough energy to take care of ourselves, to be here for ourselves, to simply be human.

There is a way, though, that can take us through these roadblocks. It is a way that leads us from the surface to the interior landscape of I-am-here-for-me. Having the awareness of how this on-the-surface part of I-am-here-for-me shows up at this particular moment is the entry point into the more subtle aspect of I-am-here-for-me.

Below the Surface With I-Am-Here-For-Me

That more subtle part of I-am-here-for-me can live just below the surface, below the awareness of reasons like: *I can't be here for me. I can't take care of myself. I just don't have the time. I don't have the energy. I'm too exhausted, even to think about it.*

At first glance, we may say that these reasons are the culprits getting in the way of our not being here for ourselves. From the vantage point of the surface of life, there's a lot of truth in reasons like these. However, exploring below the surface allows us to arrive at the truth below the truth, so to speak. Once we arrive at this deeper truth about what may or may not be going on, we can begin living life from a deeper, closer approximation of our truth. We can begin to put this truth into action, moving from simply thinking about the need to be here for ourselves to *actually* being here for ourselves, in all our humanness, in whatever way that may look.

Acceptance

The first feature to be explored in this landscape below the surface of I-am-here-for-me is acceptance. For the caregiver, this can be a confusing and scary place. I'd wager this is often the case because of a lack of clarity around what acceptance really means. It's a good idea to spend a little time taking a closer look at acceptance and what it actually is as opposed to what we may think it is.

Here's a simple way to look at acceptance. It's the process of getting real with ourselves, particularly in relation to whatever is going on in our lives as caregivers. That means getting honest with ourselves and actually acknowledging that what's happening now *is* what's happening now – nothing less, nothing more. Many people, however, equate acceptance with failure or giving up or not succeeding. In the case of the caregiver, the added dynamic of equating acceptance with not being able to save or help the person we're caring for tends to start to swirl around, too. When we give this kind of charge to acceptance, all sorts of less-than-healthy coping strategies may be activated.

It's important to remember that accepting a situation doesn't mean that you have to like the situation. It doesn't mean that you have to walk down the path of guilt, or feeling like a failure, or even feeling all-too-human. It does mean, however, that you surrender to the what-is-ness of the situation.

There is a welcoming quality about acceptance. Authentic acceptance is not forced. Rather it is a dissolving of our denial, an opening up to the experience of the situation in all its fullness. As we explore our relationship to acceptance, we may find that we're telling ourselves something along the lines of: "Fine! If I have to accept this because it is what I have to do to learn to be here for myself, then I will. I don't want to. But I will, since I have to." Words along these lines reveal not acceptance but its opposite.

If this thought process or line of reasoning rings true for us, then we're still not in the space of acceptance. It is actually an example of the thought process of someone who is forcing themselves into acceptance, which isn't really acceptance at all. It's simply another facet of the dynamic of denial, another example of a less-than-healthy coping strategy.

Taking the singular step of acceptance of our situation is liberating, whether it feels like it is or not. It is liberating because it begins to free up amazing amounts of energy for us. It is liberating also because it allows us to move more deeply into our inner landscape towards the next prominent feature of I-am-here-for-me.

Choice

Continuing to explore the inner landscape of I-am-here-for-me, we find that just beyond acceptance is the feature that we'll come to recognize as choice.

There is a certain irony that accompanies this concept of choice as it relates to the life of the caregiver. We, as caregivers, may be making hundreds of choices on any given day or during any given week for the person we're caring for. Yet we may feel like we no longer have any choice in our very own life. It may seem that all our personal power has vanished.

This is dangerous territory for any caregiver. It can cause us to fall into the robotics of simply going through the motions. It can also lead to feelings of resentment or even anger towards the person we are caring for. All of this can quickly move us into a very different place than I-am-here-for-you or I-am-here-for-me.

If we have arrived at that place of acceptance of what is actually happening in our life as caregiver, then we have arrived at that space of being able to look honestly and authentically at the situation. There's no denial. There's no false humility. There's no need to struggle with trying to make the situation anything other than it is. This is where space again starts to open up; energy again starts to flow, and we can begin to move into the arena of real choice.

Keep in mind that this act of choosing is authentic choice in the face of what is. This is in contrast to the action that masquerades as choice in the midst of denying what is. Authentic choice begins with choosing how to be. Only then can we authentically choose what to do.

Back to the Surface With I-Am-Here-For-Me

After getting clear about authentic acceptance and choice, we arrive in the space where we've finally stopped deluding ourselves. We now face life as it is, and we accept it. From this empowered place of true acceptance, we're able to make our commitment to being present for the person we're caring for actually as a result of *our* choice. We acknowledge to Life that it is our choice to be here. Because it is our choice, we can finally show up for ourselves. We can finally be here for ourselves.

We've liberated ourselves from all the falsities that may feel good, but which aren't real: false humility, false nobleness, false martyrdom. Quite simply, because we authentically choose to be here for the person we're caring for, we now can actually afford to be here for ourselves, too. We can afford to simply be human. How that looks will be different for everyone. By moving into this honest space, we can finally give ourselves permission to take care of ourselves. We can acknowledge that we are human and that we do have human needs and emotions. And it's okay to take care of those needs and emotions, even in the midst of giving care to someone else.

My brother and I split each 24-hour period.

He takes the night from about 8:30 p.m.
until 8:30 a.m.

I take the day shift from 8:30 a.m. until
about 8:30 p.m.

3

I am here with you

I have one foot inside the bathtub and one foot outside of it. I'm facing my father who is seated on the commode. He just finished peeing, which he does sitting on the commode now. My arms are under his as I bend my knees to gain enough leverage to raise him up from the commode. My father is tall: 6'2". Though he weighs only about 145 pounds right now, he is still surprisingly heavy.

Over the past several days, he has lost more strength in his legs. Where before, he could help a little as I lifted him up. That's no longer the case.

"Okay, Daddy, one, two, three." With every fiber of my body, I lift him.

As he starts to rise from the commode, "Daddy, try to lean forward some, towards me."

I'm sure he tries. But nothing happens. Finding a little more strength from God-knows-where, I finally get him into an upright position. He's unsteady, leaning on me for balance. Again, he's surprisingly heavy for his emaciated condition.

The sink is all of about one foot from the side of the commode. He puts one hand on the sink and another on my shoulder as I bend down to pull up his pajama pants.

My back is really hurting right now. I'm sweating, out of breath. I'm not sure how much longer this can continue – his using the bathroom actually in the bathroom. I feel like we're at a juncture, another unwanted turning-point.

As I step out of the tub and start to maneuvre myself to begin leading my father out of the bathroom, he stops.

He turns his body towards the small mirror hanging over the small sink. Now both of his hands are on the rim of the sink. "What are you doing, Daddy? Let's go back to your chair."

He's looking at himself in the mirror. "Hand me my brush."

I reach around him to the back of the commode, where his brush is. As I hand it to him, his shaky hand slowly takes it from me. There's a pause in time as he studies himself in the mirror as best he can. His eyesight is blurred. He squints. He opens his eyes wide. He squints again.

A moment later and he carefully brings the brush to his head. The tremor in his hand is always there. He slowly, weakly moves the brush through his hair. He makes familiar movements with it – the same ones he's made since before I was born – parting his hair to the right.

One of my arms is now around him for better support. My other hand is on his shoulder.

He finishes with the brush and shakily hands it to me. I place it on the back of the commode and return my arm to his waist.

He's not finished yet. He's still looking at himself in the mirror, studying his face, his chest, his arms. He makes a face at his reflection in the mirror – a mix of disgust, surprise, and sadness. "Look at me. I'm so *skinny*."

With my hands still supporting him, I watch.

Something shifts for me. A moment ago, I was exhausted and my back was hurting. I just wanted to get him to his chair so I could recuperate from his going to the bathroom. But now, the shift. Watching him. Being present with him. Feeling my hands hold him. With the touch of my hands I do feel his skinny body. I also feel the look he gives himself. His disgust. His surprise. His sadness. I say nothing to him. Saying anything at all would be saying something for me, not for him. Instead, I stay with him so he can stay with himself.

Simply with my touch, I let him know: I am here with you.

Dignity

Being with is the context of the journey of both this aspect of caregiving and the next. Truly being with the one we are caring for can, on the surface, seem like a bit of a no-brainer. In fact, some may jump the gun and equate it with being there *for* the one we are caring for. It's not the same journey. This being-with-you aspect of caregiving demands something more of us. It demands us to allow the person we're caring for their dignity, to allow them the dignity to have their own experience. This is at the heart of I-am-here-with-you.

If we allow this, a very paradoxical and very healing space opens up for the one we're caring for. They get the opportunity to actually be there *with* themselves. In perhaps more than any other aspect of caregiving, I-am-here-with-you is profoundly about the one we're caring for.

The door for their non-physical (and possibly physical) healing is opened by our being there *with* them. And when we make that shift from falling into one of *our* coping patterns to holding space for them to experience whatever

watch... pause... let be

it is they are experiencing (without our need to make it better – which is really for us, by the way), then we hold the door open for them to walk through to the healing potential available for them in this inner landscape of I-am-here-with-you.

Witness

Our intellectual nod to giving the person we're caring for the dignity to have their own experience is the first step towards our shifting into the role of witness. It is through our role of witness that we move into actively creating and holding space for their experience to unfold.

If we look at the act of witnessing we'll find that one of the challenges revolves around a list of not-doing's: the not-making-it-better, the not-judging, the not-getting-involved, the not-making-it-about-me, etc. The following short definition will help us get a clearer understanding of what authentic witnessing is.

> Witnessing is watching and noticing all that unfolds, without judging or changing or fixing the experience being witnessed.

Of course, if we aren't judging the experience in the first place, we'll never have the desire to change it or fix it or make it anything other than what it is.

There is another facet of witness that we need to be aware of and take part in if we are to fully support this powerful aspect of caregiving. It's the act of bearing witness. This is about speaking what is witnessed. Let's keep in mind that speaking it doesn't necessarily mean speaking words out loud. It's more akin to acknowledging what is witnessed, being a testament to it. Sometimes that can simply be silence, or a look, or a touch. These are all potent expressions of our bearing witness that can be used when spoken words don't feel right or feel like they may just get in the way.

Our honoring and participating in the whole process of authentic witness powerfully validates the experience of the one we're caring for. We support giving voice to their experience. We support letting it be heard. We support holding such a big space for it that the person we're caring for can begin to move into the realm where real healing – however that may look – may be accessed.

What Happens When We Witness

When we shift into the role of witness, we soften. We open onto experience. We expand our awareness from being solely focused on ourselves to authentically being present with the person we are caring for. We find ourselves in the space of bestowing unconditional positive regard. Without judgment in play, true witnessing naturally unfolds. It is a tender, compassionate way to be with someone. A more real way. It allows the person we are caring for to have their own experience without our getting in the way of it, no matter how much we *think* that our getting in the way is for their own good.

The Edge Experience

What if the experience becomes too big? There needs to be understanding of the situation in order to know when our being *with* them needs to shift back into the more active aspect of being there *for* them.

There is a concept known as the edge. When we move into an area where we feel heightened sensation, either physically or non-physically, we are moving into an edge for ourselves. An edge is not necessarily an unsafe space. However, the experience can move us so deeply into the edge that it can become unsafe. When this happens, we need to back away from what has become an extreme or hard edge. We need to move back into a softer edge or even leave the edge experience altogether.

As we witness the experience of the person we're caring for, if it is becoming too big, as in unsafe or life-threatening, it is time for us to move back into the I-am-here-*for*-you aspect of caregiving.

My brother and I split each 24-hour period.

He takes the night from about 8:30 p.m. until 8:30 a.m.

I take the day shift from 8:30 a.m. until about 8:30 p.m.

4

I am here
with me

I'm in the kitchen with my mother. We're out of sight of my father. We're hiding from him.

He's in his chair in the living room. My brother is kneeling on the floor in front of him.

It's about four in the afternoon. The middle of my caregiving time with my father, the middle of my brother's sleep time. I had to call him, though.

Twenty minutes earlier is a different world.

In that world, I'm sitting with my mother on the sofa in the living room. My father is in his chair opposite us. Out of the blue, my father asks where he is. He's done this before. He's had periods of being confused and even brief hallucinations. My brother started to notice a pattern between my father's pain medication and the episodes of confusion and hallucinations. Over the past several days, I've noticed this, too.

With his first question, there's something off in his tone. There's not the element of curiosity in his voice that has been present the other times.

Now more questions come in rapid fire: *Who are you? I don't have a son named Kevin. Who is she? No, she's not Joanie. She's not my wife. What have you done with Joanie? What have you done with my wife?*

We've been told different ways to handle situations like this. It's quite obvious that the approach I've just chosen to take is not the right one. But now it feels too late to change course.

Events quickly start to spiral.

I'm taking the car. I'm going to Jackson. He jumps up and grabs the car keys from the table, then lunges for the front door, opens it and starts out. Before he's too far out the door, I move him back inside and close the door. I don't know who this person is in my father's frail, weak body – a body that hasn't been able to walk or even balance on its own for weeks and weeks now.

You can't stop me. He turns and walks to the kitchen. He shuffles through drawers and grabs a large knife and a pair of scissors. *Get away from me.* He walks through the living room towards the hall, waving the knife and scissors in the air. I walk behind him. He turns. There's a wild, frightened look in his eyes. *Stay back or there's going to be blood.* He jabs the knife and scissors towards me.

I had to call my brother. I had to wake him up.

My mother and I are in the kitchen.

My brother is in the living room with my father. He's the only one who has been able to be with my father during these hallucinations, though none has ever been like this one. My brother manages to calm my father. He gets the knife, the scissors, and the car keys from him.

A nervous and unsteady waiting follows. The ambulance arrives. The paramedics take over. Then more waiting and waiting and waiting in the emergency room, the doctors and nurses, the questions and more questions, and the numbness of no real answers.

Now it's 11 p.m. We're back at the house. My father is mostly back. Tomorrow we've decided to pursue another direction to try to manage my father's pain. I'm too tired to focus on it now. I'm exhausted. We're all exhausted.

I'm in my house. I'm in my spare room, seated on a cushion on the floor. It's quiet in the house, but not in my head. It's hard to find words, but I don't feel grounded. I'm still swirling around from the afternoon's experiences. I'm still living them in my mind and in my body. Despite the exhaustion, my body feels other than tired. It feels tight. It feels scared. It feels like it has too much life experience in it. It feels overwhelmed.

As I close my eyes, I take a few breaths. It hurts to breathe. My chest is tight. My whole body is tense. I breathe a few more deep breaths. I notice that it isn't my chest that's tight. It's more my heart that hurts with each breath. I settle some. I start to move into surrender. I start to feel my body accept what is happening. I settle some more. My mind feels less crowded. A few more breaths. I shift into a welcoming space – one of knowing that I'm here with me.

Now my chest and heart start to feel less tight. They start to open up some. I recognize fear coming to the surface. I feel a hurt. It's the kind of hurt that comes from the fear and hate of a parent towards a child. My mind wants to rationalize. It wants to say it wasn't my father doing or saying those things to me. I notice my mind wanting to make everything make sense. But everything doesn't make sense.

I breathe deeply again. I hold space for myself. I am here in this space of nothing making sense. I am here with me in the hurt, in the fear, in the pain of a parent turning on a child.

As I stay with the experience, I notice the rawness of another layer: the wanting my father back. I start to sob as the emotion of yet another subtle layer comes to the surface: the wanting my father to be healthy and happy and knowing who I am.

Being With Ourselves

As we move into the I-am-here-with-you aspect of caregiving, we hold space for the person we're caring for. We allow them the dignity to have their own experience. We move into the role of witness for them. With the I-am-here-with-me aspect, we do much the same, but for ourselves. We allow ourselves the very same dignity to have our own experiences and to witness our own experiences, whatever they may be.

I-am-here-with-me, however, asks us not only to be a witness but to be an active witness. It asks us to turn an ear to the stories and experiences that live in our bodies. Parts of our experiences can stay lodged in the very cells of our bodies. Sometimes we push them there. Sometimes they simply get stuck there. If we don't listen to the story and even the story below the story, we'll find ourselves ever more stressed from the events in our lives and acting out or projecting these stories onto others, even onto the persons we're caring for.

Finding Where the Story Lives

Our stories live within us. They inhabit the cells of our bodies. Their effects can be felt in both the physical and the non-physical parts of our bodies. Let's refer to the non-physical part collectively as our mind. Usually the more stressed we are from an event in our lives, the easier it is to locate where its story lives within us.

To begin to locate the story, we need to turn to our awareness. This is the same awareness we discussed in Chapter One. How we use it is simple. We realize that we're experiencing a certain emotion or feeling. Once we've named that emotion or feeling, then we become aware of where it lives in our body. In other words, where are we experiencing the emotion or feeling in our body? Is it in our heart? Our stomach? Our head? Or somewhere else in our body? Once we know the location in our body where we're experiencing the sensations of the emotion or feeling, we move our awareness to that particular area.

Witnessing the Story

With our awareness on a particular area of our body where we're experiencing emotion or feeling, we simply shift into the role of witness for ourselves. In the process, we release any desire to judge or fix or change what we become aware of. Our intention is to open and hold space for our body so it can speak the story that is living in that particular part. We can even ask it: "What's your story?" or "What's happening now?" Then we return to silence and notice all the feelings, emotions, thoughts, images, or memories that come into our awareness. This is how our body speaks its stories. This is its language. It may use any or all of these ways to tell its stories. We simply notice all that happens. No judging. No trying to fix or change what we witness.

The Story Below the Story

Often what we become aware of seems to come to the surface of our consciousness in layers. These layers are like the story or stories below the original story. And with each layer, we become clearer about what's happening in our body. Our responsibility as witness is to remain present through as many of these layers as we can until we become aware of the root or heart of the story.

Many times we need do nothing more than remain silent and present. The layers or stories will unfold on their own. Yet there are times when we can take a more active role in this process. For example, as I become aware of a feeling of anger, I simply witness it. As I do so, I notice that it feels like there is more to this anger. So I wait in silence, in patience, and continue to witness. After some more silence, and still sensing there is something more, I decide to invite my body to fill me in on the rest of the story. I do this by saying: "Tell me more." Then I open up the space through my silent, patient witnessing. If there is more that I need to know at that time, my body will share it with me. If there is nothing else for me to hear at that time, my body will eventually become silent.

My brother and I split each 24-hour period.

He takes the night from about 8:30 p.m. until 8:30 a.m.

I take the day shift from 8:30 a.m. until about 8:30 p.m.

5

I am here

Each night for the past eight months, as I get ready to go home, I hug my father. I tell him I love him and that I'll see him in the morning. Tonight, though, I can't hug him. There's too much pain in his body. Anything other than a light touch causes the pain to flare.

As I stand by the side of his hospital bed, I survey his body. His muscles – what's left of them – are not under his control anymore. His limbs are contracted. The fingers of his hands stay curled up now. His eyes are closed. Thankfully, he seems to be resting.

Instead of hugging him goodnight, I place my finger in the curled fingers of his right hand. I tell him I love him. I wish him a good night and say that I'll see him in the morning.

He can't talk anymore. He can't open his mouth. I'm too empty, too drained, or maybe just know all too well to even expect a response. Then, without missing a beat, he squeezes my finger. It's so little. So barely noticeable. But so big.

Though it may not look like it, my father is present. He heard me. He understood me. It feels like his way of telling me he loves me. It feels like his way of wishing me a good night, his way of saying he'll see me in the morning.

Night passes.

It's 8:10 a.m.

I'm worried. I'm driving to my parents' house, and I know I'm worried. I feel it all through my body. It's not okay; I don't like this feeling. But I accept it. I don't like what this day will bring. But I accept it. This far into my caregiving experience, I realize that each step forward in time is a step that is somehow, some way, supported by something greater than myself.

It's 8:15 a.m.

I get out of my car. I'm walking to the front door. I know that today we're going to have to begin using the heavy narcotic pain medicine from hospice. I notice all the fear in my body at this thought. These types of narcotics make my father sick. He always vomits when he takes medicine like this. It's been a problem all along.

I'm at the bottom of the steps. I stop. I'm so worried that he will choke if he begins to vomit because he can't open his mouth now. My prayer this morning at the base of the steps is more of a pleading than it has ever been before: "Please, God, help."

I'm at the front door now. I take another deep breath as I turn the doorknob.

It's 8:16 a.m.

My father is sleeping in the hospital bed, which is only a few steps from the front door. My mother is on the couch next to the hospital bed. She spent the night there. My brother walks through the dining room to greet me as I close the front door.

He fills me in, just like every morning, on what has happened during the night. My father has had a relatively quiet night. It's a relief for the moment to see him sleeping. My brother tells me that he gave my father a small amount of water about a half hour ago. He used the small syringe-like tool, placing it in the corner of my father's mouth. He seemed to swallow several cc's with no problem.

It's 8:18 a.m.

In mid-sentence, my brother stops and looks at my father. We listen. He says my father's not breathing. We listen some more. My father inhales. He is breathing, but the breaths are very slow, with long pauses between each inhalation and exhalation. I tell my brother this is what happens as the body gets closer to death.

My brother moves to the side of my father's bed. I can see my own feelings of helplessness and fear in his attentive movements, in his big eyes as he watches my father.

It's 8:19 a.m.

I'm on the phone to hospice. "We have a crisis situation." I try to stay calm.

I hear my father's slow breathing while I'm on the phone. My mother is getting up now. It's hard for her. The couch is low and her knees are weak and hurt. It takes some time.

It's 8:21 a.m.

The hospice nurse is asking if my father is having difficulty breathing. I tell her no. I hear her say, "Have the medicine ready if his breathing becomes labored." I remind her of my concerns about using the medicine. She says calmly, "You don't need to worry about that." She tells me they'll be at the house soon.

It's 8:23 a.m.

I hang up and make a quick, to-the-point call to my other brother. He arrived about 10 days ago from Seattle and is staying at a nearby hotel. He answers and I tell him to get here now. We hang up.

It's 8:25 a.m

As I start to move towards the hospital bed, I hear my father make one long, easy exhalation. We all wait.

There's only silence. No inhalation. No breath.

"That's it," my brother says. "He's gone."

More silence as we let my brother's words settle on us, each in our own way.

I look at my father. No movement. No breath. No sound. No life.

On some level, I realize that I've naturally entered into an in-between experience – that space between one moment and the next. There is something most profound about in-between experiences, particularly this one. Silence expands. Liminal space opens up. Time is somehow suspended. A welcome peace moves over me. It seems incongruent, though. It seems too out of place. Part of me tries to push it away – to make the peace disappear. But it won't be pushed away. It won't leave. It overtakes this space as my mind tries to begin to process what has just happened. In this space, I feel a wholeness, a sense of being healed. My logical mind struggles.

I look around the room, saying to myself: "Where are you, Daddy? Can you see me looking for you?"

As I turn my eyes to my father's body again, my mother starts to cry. She's leaning over him, her face against his, her hands hugging his shoulders.

I drop more into the in-between space. I feel something here, some presence. I feel a something-bigger-than-me. I feel held. I feel it. And I feel it saying: "I am here."

The in-between time begins to dissolve. As it does, I notice it leaves me with the next step.

I get up and call hospice.

"My father has just passed."

In Between

It is startling how quickly, in terms of linear time, our worlds can change. In the space of 15 minutes on the morning my father passed, I stepped from one world into another. I stepped out of an uncannily familiar world with an inner landscape filled with fear, noise, struggle, and fracturedness into a world whose inner landscape was altogether new. Its newness felt odd – in part, because it was so much the opposite of the one I was just living in. It also felt odd because this new inner landscape felt so very strangely out-of-place in relation to the exterior events of the previous 15 minutes.

Between one world and another, between one exterior experience and another, exists what I call an in-between space. This in-between space exists between exterior moments. It doesn't seem to correspond or track to three-dimensional space and linear time. If we look for in-between space while operating in three-dimensional space and linear time, we struggle to find even a hint of it. In the really full or too big moments of life, however, these in-between spaces tend to open up naturally, inviting us into liminal experience.

The in-betweens, of course, exist all the time. We can learn to shift into in-between space whenever we need to integrate our exterior experiences of daily life, whenever we need the conscious support and guidance of I Am Here. For all of us who are caregivers, understanding how to access this in-between space is essential to our own healing journey.

Remembering

In-between spaces are liminal realities. There is a certain sacredness to these in-betweens. Much can take place here if we allow ourselves to receive, to open into the transcendence of the in-betweens. We touch ground here, receive revelation, and integrate our life in healthy, healing ways. We often move out of in-betweens with a greater understanding and knowing our next step for holistically integrating our life experience.

Entering into our in-betweens at will often begins by a remembering. This remembering is not just an exercise of intellect. Rather it's a whole-body remembering. We take time to turn inward, recollecting our day and calling back to mind and body the awareness that seems to be most prominent. As we stand before this awareness, we notice how it either shows up in our life or not. Then we turn more inward, this time towards our heart space. With each breath, we settle more deeply into ourselves, into our heart space. We move towards the threshold of in-between. We open up to liminal space. We open up to the presence of I-Am-Here, in all its wisdom and all its compassion and all its love.

In this liminal space, we rest. We bring with us our awareness and whatever is standing out for us and then we rest and open ourselves to guidance, however it may show up or be revealed. We can stay here in the in-between for as long as we like – resting, receiving, and being held and supported.

As we feel ready, we can start to move back into our linear space and time by simply asking: What now or what next do I do? Then in the same manner that we opened ourself up to the wisdom of this liminal space, we open ourself up to receiving the answer to this question. After we become aware of the answer, we begin to shift our awareness to our breathing, then to our body. Next we slowly open our eyes, taking some time to reconnect with our exterior world.

After an in-between experience, we are different. How we are different may be subtle, but this doesn't take away from its significance. When I return from my in-between experiences, I feel more whole, more integrated, softer, peaceful, even held and supported – knowing in that whole-body way that I'm not alone in all of this. No matter how big my caregiving life becomes, I can fall back again and again into that eternal presence that ever calls out: I Am Here.

Epilogue

The right question

In the introduction, I wrote that I had been asking myself the wrong question during the initial months of my caregiving experience with my father. I had been asking: "When will it stop?" Not a bad question to want to know the answer to. Just not the question that invites as well as allows peace and tenderness and healing to wash over us and infuse our experiences.

When will it stop? is a question that speaks so much about the questioner. It usually points towards a stress-filled, fractured, painful inner landscape. It reveals a questioner who may be experiencing exhaustion, isolation, even desperation. Unfortunately, it is never the question that will lead to the inner landscape. It will never lead us into the healing journey of caregiving.

The question that will take us to that liminal space of transformation is one that is just as brief, but exponentially more powerful. We simply need to ask ourselves *What's happening now?* instead of *When will it stop?*

We can consciously access liminal, in-between space only when we are in our bodies in the present moment. This is, of course, as opposed to being in our minds in the future, running away from the present. This is exactly why *What's happening now?* is so powerful. It immediately takes us out of the future and brings us back to the present.

What's happening now? settles us. It allows us to move more deeply into our inner landscape. It opens us to the act of witnessing. It supports us so we can listen to the stories in our body. It grounds us so we can go deeper, listening to the stories beneath the stories.

As we do this, we find ourselves in the middle of being held. We find ourselves touching that place of wisdom that is at the heart of each of us, caregiver or not.

It is here that we receive healing, in the in-between. It is here that we receive peace. It is here that we find ourselves supported in ways beyond which any words can convey.

And it all starts with a simple question – one that doesn't project us into some future, but one that brings us squarely into our very own body, in our very own present moment.

So, if you're ready. . .

What's happening now?

Made in United States
North Haven, CT
01 July 2022

20867371R00050